Write It Right

Writing a Comic Book

By Cecilia Minden

Published in the United States of America by
Cherry Lake Publishing
Ann Arbor, Michigan
www.cherrylakepublishing.com

Reading Adviser: Marla Conn MS, Ed., Literacy specialist, Read-Ability, Inc.
Book Designer: Felicia Macheske
Character Illustrator: Carol Herring

Photo Credits: © George Rudy/Shutterstock, 7; © Africa Studio/Shutterstock, 15

Graphics Throughout: © simple surface/Shutterstock.com; © Mix3r/Shutterstock.com; © Artefficient/Shutterstock.com; © lemony/Shutterstock.com; © Svetolk/Shutterstock.com; © EV-DA/Shutterstock.com; © briddy/Shutterstock.com; © IreneArt/Shutterstock.com

Copyright © 2020 by Cherry Lake Publishing
All rights reserved. No part of this book may be reproduced or utilized in any
form or by any means without written permission from the publisher.

Library of Congress Cataloging-in-Publication Data has been filed and is available at catalog.loc.gov

Cherry Lake Publishing would like to acknowledge the work of The Partnership for 21st Century Skills.
Please visit www.p21.org for more information.

Printed in the United States of America
Corporate Graphics

Table of CONTENTS

CHAPTER ONE
Be a Super Storyteller! 4

CHAPTER TWO
Tips from the Pros 6

CHAPTER THREE
Creating Characters 8

CHAPTER FOUR
Telling Your Story 12

CHAPTER FIVE
Putting It All Together 16

GLOSSARY 22
FOR MORE INFORMATION 23
INDEX 24
ABOUT THE AUTHOR 24

CHAPTER ONE

Be a Super Storyteller!

When was the last time you read a comic book? Comic books are a great way to tell interesting stories. They can contain many words or have no words at all. Comic books can be funny or sad. Some are printed in color. Others are in black and white. Comic books can tell **fictional** stories or describe real-life events.

All comic books use pictures. The pictures are arranged in an order that tells a story. The pictures show readers what your characters look like. They can look like real people or come totally from your imagination.

The text on a comic book page is called lettering. Most comic book lettering is written in CAPITAL LETTERS. Important words are put in **bold** lettering. Large lettering is used for shouting. Small lettering means characters are whispering.

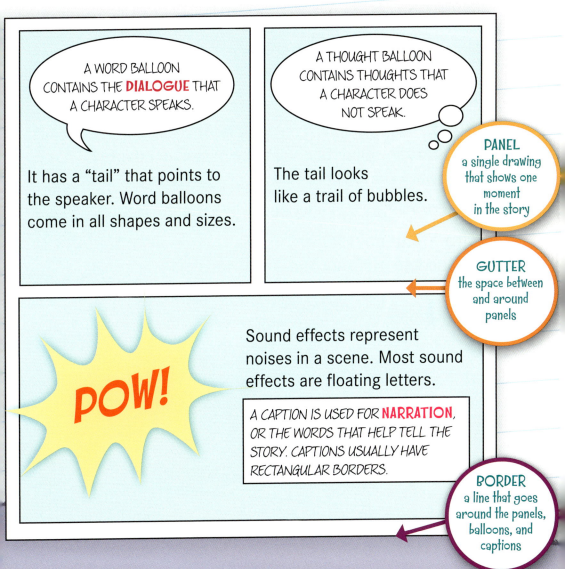

CHAPTER TWO

Tips from the Pros

You can write a comic book about anything you can imagine. Here are a few writing tips before you begin:

- Learn from the pros. Pay careful attention when you're watching a movie or a TV show. Does the dialogue sound like it comes from real life? Did the **plot** make sense?

- Create interesting, original characters. They should be colorful and **unique** in some way. Make the characters the kind your readers will want to get to know.

- Write about things that interest you. That makes it easier for you to create characters and dialogue.

- Write about things you know. If you need more information, research the subject at the library or online.

- Don't stop writing. Writing becomes easier the more you do it. Write every day until it becomes a habit.

- Keep at it! Your first comics might not be what you want. Keep trying ideas until you can write with ease.

ACTIVITY

Getting Started

Come up with some ideas for a story. Think of books and movies you've enjoyed.

INSTRUCTIONS:

1. Draw a line down the middle of a piece of notebook paper.
2. Write "Ideas I liked" at the top of the left side. Write "Ideas I would like to explore" at the top of the right side.
3. Under "Ideas I liked," make a list of the things you liked in books or movies.
4. Under "Ideas I would like to explore," make a list of the things you're interested in but don't know a lot about.
5. You'll need to research these subjects if you want to write a story about them.

CHAPTER THREE

Creating Characters

You've decided what you want to write about. Now it's time to think about who you're writing about. Your **script** describes each panel and page of your comic. It contains all of the dialogue and captions. To write a script, you need characters.

Your characters must be believable. They should face problems. They should have feelings and **goals** just like real people do. We should want to read about their **relationships**. These relationships give readers a lot of information. They tell what the characters are like and where they came from.

Every person in real life is different. Each of your characters should also be different. One character may be neat, while another one is sloppy. Maybe one character has special powers and another is a bully.

Give each character a **conflict**. Conflict is the main ingredient of an interesting story. Each character has goals. Conflict is something that stands in the way of these goals. Conflict that seems real will help make your characters believable.

Do you have favorite comic book characters?

ACTIVITY

Make a Chart

You've thought about your characters. Now you need to organize your thoughts. A chart can help you do this. Look at the chart on page 11. It shows one way to describe a character in a comic book story. Make a similar chart for each of your comic book characters.

HERE'S WHAT YOU'LL NEED:

- Notebook paper
- Ruler
- Pencil

INSTRUCTIONS:

1. Use a ruler to help you draw four boxes on a piece of paper.
2. Label your chart in the same way as the boxes on page 11.
3. Fill in the boxes with information about your character.

Sample Comic Book Chart

TITLE: Super Cat and Rudy Rat
AUTHOR: Amelia
NAME OF CHARACTER: Super Cat/Max

BACKGROUND INFORMATION
- A 10-pound (4.5 kilogram) orange cat
- Family calls him Max
- Super Cat identity is secret
- Flies when there are no humans around
- Rudy Rat is sworn enemy

PERSONALITY
- Likes to take long naps in a sunny window
- Does not like his naps interrupted
- Is very brave and becomes Super Cat when he sees injustice

WHAT HE WANTS
- To stop Rudy Rat from interrupting his naps
- To send Rudy Rat far, far away
- To take a long nap in a sunny window

WHAT'S IN HIS WAY (conflict)
- Rudy Rat, who loves to tease Super Cat and wake him up

CHAPTER FOUR

Telling Your Story

The stories in most comic books are divided into a beginning, middle, and end. This type of storytelling is called a three-act structure. The beginning is called the first act. It introduces the main characters and the main conflict. It also describes the **setting**. The middle is called the second act. It adds further challenges for the characters. This increases the feeling of **suspense** in the story. The third act is the end. It presents the main solution to the conflict. It shows how characters and situations have changed throughout the story. This is the thrilling conclusion of the story.

ACTIVITY

Making a Chart

Map out the three acts of your story before you start writing your script.

HERE'S WHAT YOU'LL NEED:

- Notebook paper
- Ruler
- Pencil

INSTRUCTIONS:

1. Use a ruler to help you draw three large boxes on the paper.
2. Label the boxes "Act I," "Act II," and "Act III."
3. Write the name of your story and your name above the boxes.
4. Fill in the boxes with information about your story.

You can put in as many details as you wish. Include some dialogue and captions. Explain what you want drawn in certain panels. Including more information will make it easier to write your final script.

Sample Comic Book Chart

TITLE: Super Cat and Rudy Rat
AUTHOR: Amelia

THREE-ACT STRUCTURE:

ACT I

- We see a large orange cat curled up on a sunny window ledge.
- We hear lots of noise outside the window that wakes up the cat.
- Act I ends with an angry cat slipping out the cat door. He is going to take care of whoever woke him up.

ACT II

- The cat, named Max, gets to the yard. He sees Rudy Rat going through the garbage and making lots of noise.
- Max turns into Super Cat! He is now flying over the garbage cans.
- Rudy Rat sees him. He throws garbage at Super Cat to try and bring him down.
- A can hits Super Cat, and he falls to the ground.

ACT III

- Super Cat is on the ground as Rudy Rat approaches.
- Rudy Rat is laughing as he stands over the cat.
- Suddenly, Super Cat springs to his feet and catches the rat! He picks him up and flies him deep into the forest. Then he drops the rat.
- The last scene is a large orange cat asleep on the sunny window ledge.

Be creative and have fun!

CHAPTER FIVE

Putting It All Together

You've worked out the rough plot of your story. You've created your characters. Now it's time to put it all together and start writing.

Start by describing the settings where the action takes place. Be as specific as you can. Is it a big city or a small town? Is it morning or nighttime? Is there rain, snow, or sun? Write lots of details to keep your readers interested.

Find clever ways to move from scene to scene while continuing the mood of your story. Some writers use dialogue or captions to do this.

Every comic book script must contain art directions. They help the artist who's going to draw the story. Describe what should be in each panel. This includes the setting and what the characters are doing. Art directions also describe characters' clothes, emotions, and any other details you can think of.

Should the panel be a close-up? Close-ups are a great way to show emotion or strong drama. Should the panel be a medium shot? Medium shots are good for showing where characters are positioned in the setting. A long shot is good for introducing a new setting. Mix up your selection of shots as you write your script. This will help to vary the mood of your story.

Comic Book Script

TITLE: Super Cat and Rudy Rat
AUTHOR: Amelia

Page 1
Panel 1

Art directions: One big panel, called a splash page, showing a big orange cat curled up on a wide window ledge. Bright, sunny day.

Caption: Max loved nothing more than a long nap on a sunny windowsill.

Caption: The nap was ended by Max's enemy Rudy Rat, the rudest rat in town.

Page 2

Sound effects: CRASH! BOOM!

Panel 1

Art directions: Long shot. Max opens one eye with a very angry expression on his face. We see the opening to the kitchen where there is a cat door. Max's owner is not seen.

Max's owner DIALOGUE: I think there might be a raccoon in the trash can.

Panel 2

Art directions: Close-up of Max as he heads for the cat door.

Max DIALOGUE: I'll find out who ended my sunny nap!

Comic Book Script (Continued)

PANEL 3

Art directions: Max runs to the garbage can. Trash is flying out as Rudy digs for food. There is litter all over the ground. We see a long tail over the rim of the can.

Balloon pointer to can: Rudy DIALOGUE: I know there is cheese in here. I can smell it.

Max thought balloon: That is no raccoon. That is Rudy, the rudest rat in town.

PANEL 4

Art directions: Max is now behind a tree. He has turned into Super Cat. He is wearing a tiger-striped outfit with a big cape. The cape becomes wings so he can fly. He has a fierce expression on his face. Rudy is in the garbage can and is laughing.

Balloon over the can: Rudy DIALOGUE: Ha! Found it! That lazy cat is still sleeping in the window while I'm stealing his trash. Ha! Ha!

Max DIALOGUE: It is time for Super Cat to rid our town of Rudy, the rudest rat in town.

ACTIVITY

Finishing Your Comic Book Script

Now it's time to put your finished script together. Take a look at the sample on the previous spread before you begin.

INSTRUCTIONS:

1. Go to the top of the first page of your script. Write the name of your story, your name, and the artist's name there.
2. For each panel, provide art directions for the artist.
3. Write the dialogue, captions, and sound effects that you want in each panel.
4. Make sure your script has a beginning, middle, and end. This is important even if your script is short. Your story should have a lot of drama and conflict to keep readers interested.
5. Read your script after you've finished writing. This will help you find mistakes or places where you can improve your story.

Now you know how to create a comic book! Have a lot of fun imagining new stories to tell. Share with friends to get their input.

Good luck—and happy comic book writing!

GLOSSARY

conflict (KAHN-flikt) struggle or disagreement

dialogue (DYE-uh-lawg) conversation, especially in a book, play, movie, or TV show

fictional (FIK-shuh-nuhl) made up

goals (GOHLZ) things you are trying to accomplish

narration (na-RAY-shuhn) words describing the things that are happening in a story

plot (PLAHT) the main story of a comic book or any other work of fiction

relationships (rih-LAY-shuhn-ships) the ways people feel about and behave toward one another

script (SKRIPT) the written text that describes all the details of a comic book story

setting (SET-ing) the time period and location where a story takes place

suspense (suh-SPENS) a nervous and uncertain feeling caused by not knowing what might happen next

unique (yoo-NEEK) being the only one of its kind, unlike anything else

For More INFORMATION

BOOKS

Roche, Art. *Comic Strips: Create Your Own Comic Strips from Start to Finish*. New York, NY: Sterling, 2011.

Rosinsky, Natalie M. *Graphic Novel*. Minneapolis, MN: Compass Point Books, 2009.

WEBSITES

MyKidsAdventures—How to Create a Comic Strip
http://www.mykidsadventures.com/create-comic-strip-kids
Use seven easy steps to create a comic strip.

HowStuffWorks—How Comic Books Work
http://entertainment.howstuffworks.com/arts/comic-books/comic-book.htm
Read how comic books have made a huge impact on American culture.

INDEX

art directions, 17

balloons, 5

captions, 5, 8, 16
characters, 6, 8–12, 17
chart, 10–11, 13–14
comic books
   script writing, 16–21
   tips from pros, 6
   what they are, 4–7

conclusion, 12
conflict, 9, 12

dialogue, 5, 6, 8, 16

lettering, 5

mood, 16, 17

panels, 5, 8, 17
pictures, 4

research, 6

script, 8, 16–21
setting, 12, 16, 17
storytelling, 4–7, 12–15
suspense, 12

three-act structure, 12–14

About the AUTHOR

Cecilia Minden, PhD, is the former director of the Language and Literacy Program at Harvard Graduate School of Education. She earned her doctorate from the University of Virginia. Her research focused on early literacy skills and developing phonics curriculums. She is currently a literacy consultant and the author of over 100 books for children. Dr. Minden would like to thank Juliette Blishen for her help with this book.